Never Long Enough

Finding comfort and hope
amidst grief and loss

Rabbi Joseph H. Kra[...]

Dr. Michelle Y. Sider

ISBN: 978-1-942011-78-1
Version 1.0

Contact Rabbi Joseph H. Krakoff: jkrakoff@JewishHospice.org
Contact Dr. Michelle Y. Sider: michellesider@gmail.com

Published by Skywardjems, LLC

Cover art and illustrations by Dr. Michelle Y. Sider

For information about customized editions, bulk purchases or permissions, contact Front Edge Publishing at info@FrontEdgePublishing.com

Publishing services by Front Edge Publishing, LLC (info@FrontEdgePublishing.com)

Produced and published in the U.S.A.

Dedication from Joseph:

I truly cherish the time I get to spend with my incredible family although it is never long enough. I dedicate this book to each of them and express my appreciation for their encouragement, support and unconditional love. To my loving wife Susan and three precious children Atara, Micah and Elan – I love you and feel truly blessed to have you in my life. Additionally, I have profound gratitude for the Almighty Who gives me the strength to perform holy work each and every day.

Dedication from Michelle:

To my talented, supportive and loving husband, Bill and my three amazing sons, Joshua, Eli and Benjamin, this book is dedicated to you, for I put my heart into my art and you are my heart. Thank you for encouraging and inspiring me to be my very best. I am truly grateful for the privilege of using my God-given abilities to help others.

This book is presented to:

_____

Life is precious, irreplaceable and seems to go by far too quickly.

While this book was primarily created to help you find comfort, consolation and support in the precious recollections you have of your loved one, it can also be used to facilitate conversation around life review. It is our hope that each page will generate a new opportunity for reflection and discussion.

The loss of a loved one is painful, poignant and significant. The relationships we form endure beyond the length of our days. When we lose a dear one to death, it does not have to be the end of our connection to them. They leave behind a treasure of cherished memories that no one can ever take away.

In this spirit we have provided blank pages at the back of this book for personal memories and reflections. When we remember a loved one, their legacy becomes eternal.

Where have the years gone?

It feels like only last month

we were sharing

laughing

and guarding each other's
precious thoughts

Where have the years gone?

It feels like only last week

we were holding one
another lovingly

and anticipating our future

Where have the years gone?

It feels like only yesterday

we were vibrant and young

pursuing life's every
dream and possibility

celebrate

movement

discovering

glow of youth

freedom

on the Run

Live the life you've imagined.

Introducing

your dreams

an exciting new destination

GOING

Next Adventure

PLACES

vealing the brightness

And today

I am focused on memories of the past

reflecting on the time
we had together

the endless joys we shared

and wishing we had

just one more
day

If only we could share
one last word

one last smile

one last touch

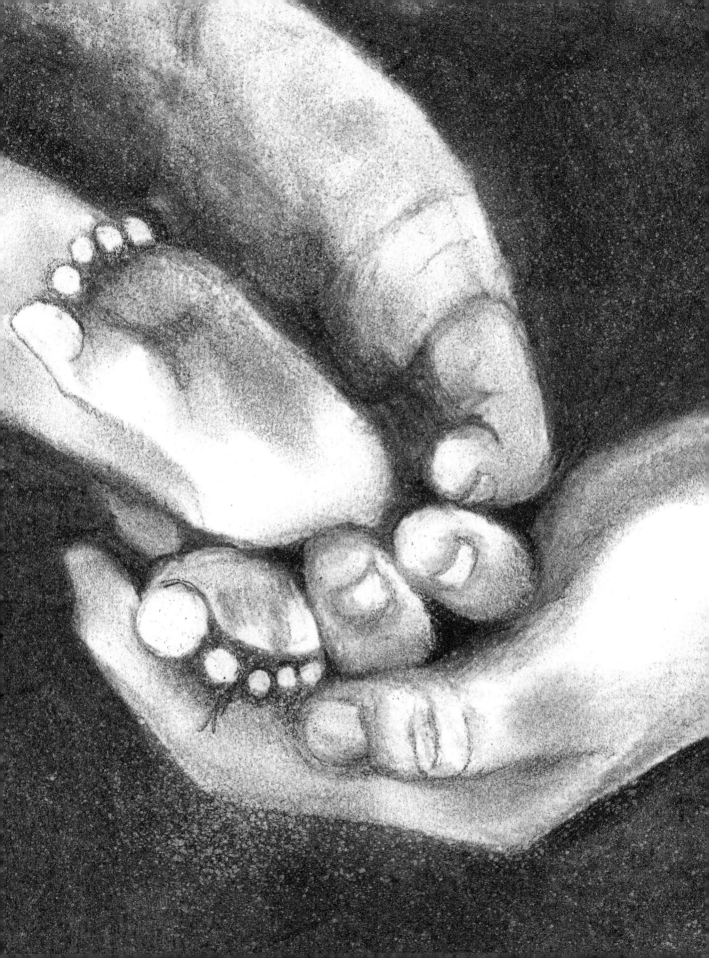

one more hug...

one final kiss.

The truth is that life is

Never

Long

Enough

There are never
enough years

Yet I will forever
be thankful
we had each other

Those beautiful and
cherished memories

will be written on
my heart forever

For nothing
and no one

can ever take them
away from me

Not
even

Time...

Memories & Reflections

Memories & Reflections

Memories & Reflections

Memories & Reflections

 **Dr. Michelle Y. Sider** is a freelance artist and art teacher in Metro Detroit. She is an illustrator and her art work includes: paintings, drawings, ketubot, glass mosaics, furniture and museum exhibits. Her background as both an artist and psychologist provide a unique perspective with which to approach projects aimed at healing and teaching. Working as an artist, teacher, psychologist and art therapist, Dr. Sider has had the privilege of helping many individuals.

Dr. Sider, a native Detroiter, received her B.F.A. from the University of Michigan in Ann Arbor, Michigan and a M.A. and Ph.D. in clinical psychology from the University of Detroit in Detroit, Michigan. She began her career as a fine artist, worked as a clinical psychologist and later returned to her art career as both teacher and artist.

Dr. Sider is married to Bill and has three children, Joshua, Eli and Benjamin.

 **Rabbi Joseph H. Krakoff** is the Senior Director of the Jewish Hospice and Chaplaincy Network. He offers educational classes and seminars to teenagers and adults on a variety of spiritual topics with a particular focus on moral and ethical behavior, palliative care and end of life decision-making.

Growing up in Los Angeles, he earned his Bachelor of Arts Degree at Bucknell University in Lewisburg, PA. An ordained Conservative Rabbi, he earned a Masters Degree of Hebrew Letters at the University of Judaism in Los Angeles, CA, and a Masters of Hebrew Letters at the Jewish Theological Seminary in New York City where he was ordained in 1998. After serving as a congregational rabbi for sixteen years, Rabbi Krakoff continues to actively participate in a whole host of lifecycle events while helping individuals and families realize their best selves.

Rabbi Krakoff is married to Susan and has three children, Atara, Micah and Elan.

In Loving Memory:

Jennifer Lanxner (1975-2015)

 Jennifer Lanxner, a friend and colleague, always counted her blessings. Since childhood she wanted to be a teacher and she became a teacher extraordinaire—profoundly devoted, dedicated and committed to her students and fellow teachers alike. Her smile was infectious and lit up every room she entered. Her personality was engaging and she always strived to do the right thing. Jennifer embodied the true essence of sweetness, kindness and unconditional love. The world is a sadder place without her in it. We remember how deeply Jennifer touched our lives.

We will forever miss her.

CPSIA information can be obtained
at www.ICGtesting.com
Printed in the USA
LVOW05s0011140517
534452LV00001B/1/P

9 781942 011781